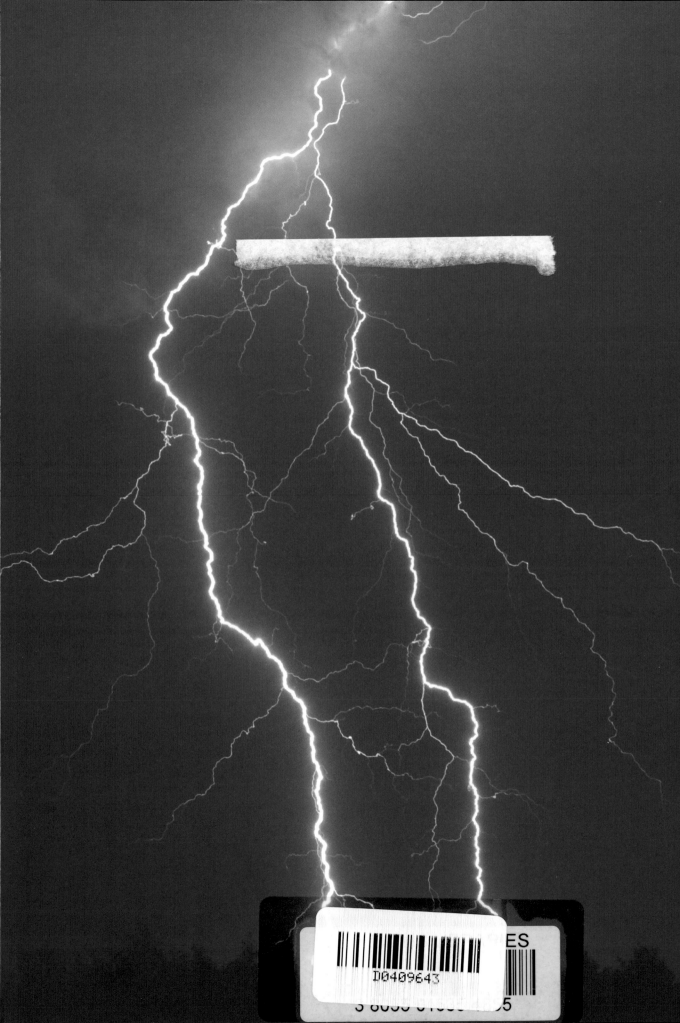

FIRST SCIENCE LIBRARY
Magnets & Sparks

- 16 EASY-TO-FOLLOW EXPERIMENTS FOR LEARNING FUN
- FIND OUT HOW ELECTRICITY AND MAGNETISM WORK!

WENDY MADGWICK

ARMADILLO

~~~~~~

This edition is published by Armadillo,
an imprint of Anness Publishing Ltd, 108 Great Russell Street,
London WC1B 3NA; info@anness.com

www.annesspublishing.com

If you like the images in this book and would like to investigate using
them for publishing, promotions or advertising, please visit our website
www.practicalpictures.com for more information.

© Anness Publishing Ltd 2014

Publisher: Joanna Lorenz
Designer: Anita Ruddell
Illustrations: Catherine Ward/Simon Girling Associates
Photographer: Andrew Sydenham
Thanks to Aneesah, Luke, May and William for appearing in the book
Production Controller: Mai-Ling Collyer

PUBLISHER'S NOTE
Although the advice and information in this book are believed to be
accurate and true at the time of going to press, neither the authors nor
the publisher can accept any legal responsibility or liability for any
errors or omissions that may have been made nor for any inaccuracies
nor for any loss, harm or injury that comes about from following
instructions or advice in this book.

Words that appear in **bold** in the text are explained in the glossary
on page 32.

Manufacturer: Anness Publishing Ltd, 108 Great Russell Street,
London WC1B 3NA, England
For Product Tracking go to: www.annesspublishing.com/tracking
Batch: 7008-22866-1127

Contents

Looking at magnets and electricity

This book has lots of fun activities to help you find out about magnets and electricity. Here are some simple rules you should follow before doing an activity.

- Always tell a grown-up what you are doing and ask if you can do the activity.
- Always read through the activity before you start it. Collect all the materials you will need.
- Make sure you have enough space to set up your activity.
- Follow the steps carefully and do exactly what you are told.
- Ask a grown-up to strip the plastic off electrical wires and to help you cut things.
- Watch what happens carefully.
- Look after your magnets. Try not to drop them. When you are not using them, put a piece of steel across the ends. Or stick your magnets together in pairs.
- Use a 4.5 volt battery with clear terminals for these experiments. **NEVER** use larger batteries or car batteries as this can be dangerous.
- **NEVER TOUCH MAINS ELECTRICITY SOCKETS OR PLUGS.**
- Never put a magnet very near to a watch, clock, computer or television screen.
- Keep a notebook. Draw pictures or write down what you did and what happened during the activity.
- Always clear up when you have finished. Wash your hands.

▶ When **static electricity** passes from one thundercloud to another or to the ground, we see a flash of **lightning**.

Magic magnets

A magnet is a piece of iron or steel that draws things towards it. We say it **attracts** an object. Let's find out what things a magnet attracts.

Stick or stay?

Collect small things made from different materials as in the picture.

Put the end of the magnet near each object. Which ones stick to the magnet?

A magnet attracts things made from steel and iron. It will not attract things made from other materials. It does not attract all metals.

Flying butterfly

1 Cut out a picture of a butterfly from a magazine. Tie a piece of thread to a paper clip. Tape the paper clip to the back of the paper butterfly.

2 Tape the other end of the thread to the edge of a table.

3 Bring your magnet close to the butterfly. Slowly move the magnet away. What happens to the butterfly? The magnet attracts the paper clip and the butterfly rises into the air.

Make a few more butterflies. Find out how high each butterfly will fly. How far away can you move the magnet before each butterfly falls?

Lift up!

Some magnets are stronger than others. Strong magnets have more pulling power than weak magnets. How strong are your magnets? Let's find out.

Pulling power

Put some paper clips on a flat surface. Pick up a paper clip with a magnet. How many paper clips can you pick up at one time? Repeat with a different magnet.

The strongest magnet will pick up the most paper clips.

▶ We can use magnets and paper clips to make a fun fishing game.

Let's fish

You will need: paper clips, two magnets, kitchen foil, round-ended scissors, bowl of water, two small magnets, thread, two thin sticks, a friend to join in!

1 Cut out some fish shapes from kitchen foil. Push a paper clip on to each fish.

2 Tie a piece of thread about 30cm/12in long to a small magnet. Tie the other end of the thread to a thin stick. Tape it in place.

3 Put the foil fish in a bowl of water. Try to catch the fish with your magnet fishing rod. The player who picks up the most fish is the winner.

Move it!

Magnets can attract things through water and through some solid objects.

Sail away

You will need: pencil, thin cardboard, round-ended scissors, cork (ask a grown-up to cut it in half), two wooden cocktail sticks or toothpicks, four drawing pins (thumb tacks), magnet, stick, shallow plastic tray, magazines, water.

3 Tape a magnet to a small ruler or stick.

1 Draw two sail shapes on cardboard. Cut them out.

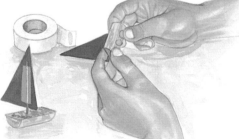

2 Tape a wooden stick to each sail. Push the pointed end of each stick into the cork halves. Push two pins into the bottom of each cork boat.

4 Put a shallow plastic tray on two piles of magazines of the same height. Pour in some water and float your boats.

5 Push the magnet under the tray. Move the magnet around to move your boats.

Diving doll

You will need: non-hardening clay, two paper clips, jar, strong magnet.

1 Make a small doll from clay. Press two paper clips into its back, one on top of the other.

2 Put your doll in a jar. Make sure its back is towards the outside of the jar.

3 Slide a magnet up the side of the jar by the doll. The magnet attracts the paper clips. As you move the magnet it pulls up the doll.

Push or pull?

Magnets have two ends, or poles.
One end is called the north pole.
The other is called the south pole.

North or south?

You can use a **compass** to find the north pole of a magnet.

You will need: thread, two bar magnets, poster paints, compass.

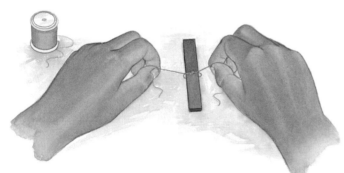

1 Tie a thread around the middle of a magnet.

2 Hang the magnet from a table. When the magnet stops moving, use a compass to find which end is pointing north. Paint the north pole red and the south pole green.

3 Bring the north pole of one magnet near the south pole of another magnet.

4 Bring two magnets' north poles close to each other. What happens to the magnets when you do this?

North and south poles attract each other. The two magnets come together. Like poles **repel** each other. This means that two north poles or two south poles push each other away.

Flying planes

You will need: cardboard, round-ended scissors, two small magnets, sticky tape.

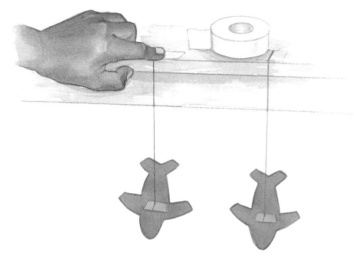

1 Draw two aircraft shapes on cardboard. Cut them out. Tape a small magnet underneath each plane. The north poles must point to the nose of each plane.

2 Tape a thread 30cm/12in long to the middle of each plane. Hang the planes about 20cm/8in apart from the side of a table. Make sure they are pointing towards you.

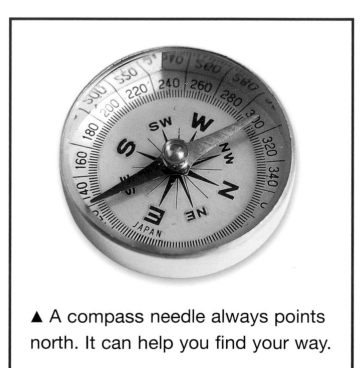

▲ A compass needle always points north. It can help you find your way.

3 Gently tap the nose of one plane towards the nose of the other plane. What happens?

The planes keep swinging to and fro.

Magnetic Earth

The Earth behaves as if there is a giant bar magnet running through its middle from pole to pole. If you hold a magnet so that it can rotate freely, it always ends up with one end pointing to the Earth's North Pole and the other to the South Pole. This is how a compass works – the needle swings to the North.

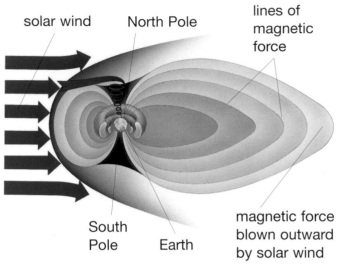

solar wind North Pole lines of magnetic force

South Pole Earth

magnetic force blown outward by solar wind

▲ Magnetic shield

The Earth's magnetic field extends about 65,000km/40,000 miles into space. It protects us from solar wind from the sun.

Which way up?

We are so familiar with maps having north at the top, that they look odd when they are turned around. Can you recognize this country (left) when it is upside down? Can you find it on a globe (right)?

Make a compass

You can create your own compass using a needle and a magnet.

You will need: steel needle, bar magnet, slice of cork, sticky tape, small bowl, water.

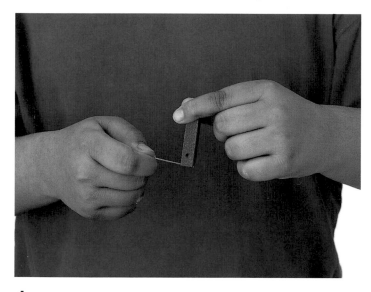

1 To turn the needle into a magnet, stroke the end of the magnet slowly along it. Repeat this in the same direction for about 45 seconds. This magnetizes the needle.

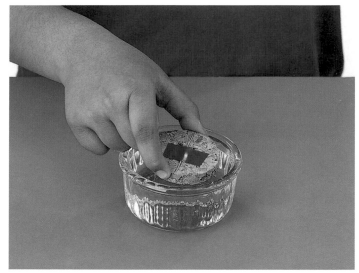

3 Fill the bowl nearly to the brim with water, and float the cork in it. Make sure the cork is exactly in the middle and can turn around without catching on the edges of the bowl.

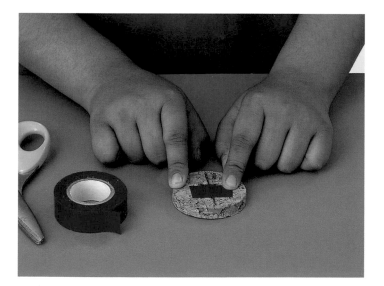

2 Place the magnetized needle on the slice of cork. Make sure that it is exactly in the middle, otherwise it will not spin evenly. Tape the needle into place.

The Earth's magnetic field should now swivel the needle on the cork. One end of the needle will always point to the north. That end is its north pole.

Fancy fields

A magnet has a special area around it called a **magnetic field**. Inside this field a magnet has pulling power. This field is invisible but we can see it in other ways.

Pretty patterns

You will need: two bar magnets, paper, iron filings, pencil.

1 Put a magnet on a table. Place a sheet of paper over it. Sprinkle iron filings over the paper.

2 Tap the paper gently. What happens to the iron filings? The iron filings are attracted to the magnet and form a pattern. This pattern shows what the magnetic field looks like.

End to end

What happens to the magnetic field when you bring two magnets together?

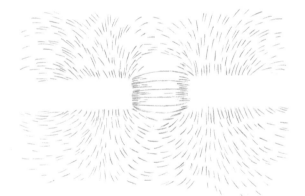

1 Put two magnets on a table. Put one magnet's north pole about 5cm/2in away from the other's south pole.

3 Try this again with the south poles of the two magnets facing each other. Is the pattern different?

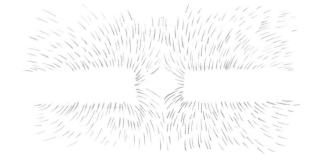

When a north pole faces a south pole the iron filings form lines between them.

2 Put a sheet of paper on top of the magnets. Slowly sprinkle on some iron filings. Tap the paper gently. What pattern do the iron filings make? Draw a picture of the pattern.

When two south poles face each other the iron filings bend away from the poles.

On end

When some objects are rubbed together, they build up static electricity. These objects then have an **electric charge**.

You will need: balloon, balloon pump, nylon material, water, towel, wool, cotton material, wood, kitchen foil.

Hair raising

Make sure your hair is clean and dry. Rub your hair several times with a balloon. Now bring the balloon near to your hair. What happens? Your hair should stand on end!

The hair and the balloon become charged with static electricity. Your hair has an opposite charge to the balloon. The charge on your hair is attracted to the charge on the balloon.

Balloon power

Can you make a balloon stick to a wall on its own?

1 Blow up a balloon with a pump. Knot the end. Put the balloon against the wall. Let it go. What happens?

2 Now rub the balloon 20 times with a piece of nylon. Hold the part of the balloon you rubbed against the wall. What happens now?

3 Wet the balloon and rub it with the nylon. Put the balloon against the wall. What happens?

4 Dry the balloon. Rub the balloon 20 times with other dry, clean materials. Try wool, cotton, wood and kitchen foil. Which materials make the balloon stick to the wall?

19

Charges and sparks

Static electricity can build up in an object. It can pass from one object to another as a spark of electricity. It can also leak away.

Move over!

You will need: two balloons, balloon pump, thread, nylon material.

1 Blow up two balloons. Tie a piece of thread to each balloon. Hold up the balloons about 20cm/8in apart. Do the balloons move?

2 Rub each balloon 20 times with nylon.

3 Hold up the balloons with the rubbed sides next to each other. What happens?

4 Hold the balloons still for a few seconds. Watch what happens.

The rubbed balloons will move apart. When you leave the balloons the charge leaks away. The balloons fall back down.

Lift off

Can you pick up paper with a pen?

You will need: tissue paper, round-ended scissors, clean plastic pen.

1 Cut some tissue paper into 1cm/½in squares. Put a clean plastic pen near the paper. What happens to the paper?

2 Rub the pen hard five times with nylon material. Put it near to the paper. What happens now?

3 Rub the pen 20 times. Does it pick up more paper?

4 Leave the pen for two minutes. Can you pick up as much paper as before?

The more you rub the pen, the more paper it will pick up. After two minutes, you will not be able to pick up so much paper.

◀ Lightning is a flash of static electricity which passes from a thundercloud to another cloud or to the ground.

21

Power stores

When electricity flows along a wire we call it an **electric current**. Electricity is used to run machines. It can be stored in a **battery**. Batteries are used to make things work.

▲ The electricity in your home flows from a **power station** along big wires. Do you know which machines in this picture use electricity?

Battery power

These things use batteries to make them work. Can you think of other things that use batteries?

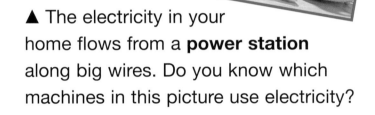

Light up

Let's see how a torch (flashlight) works.

1 Look at a torch. Make sure the switch is off. Is the bulb lit up? Ask a grown-up to help you take the torch to pieces. Look at all the parts.

2 Ask a grown-up to put the torch back together. Switch it on. What happens?

3 Open the end of the torch. Take out the batteries. Put the end back on the torch and switch it on. What happens?

4 Put the batteries back in. Take out the bulb. Put the end back on. Switch on the torch. What happens?

Your torch will only light up when the battery and bulb are there and the switch is on.

Wired up!

In a torch the battery, switch and bulb are connected by wires to make a **circuit**. Electricity flows from the battery along wires and lights the bulb.

Light circuits

You will need: 90cm/35in electrical flex, six paper clips, round-ended scissors, battery, bulb, bulb holder, metal coat hanger, 25cm/10in stiff wire.

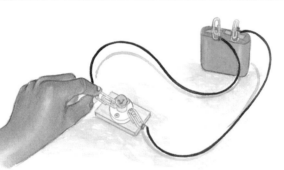

3 Put the bulb in the bulb holder. Attach pieces of flex to the bulb holder as shown. Does the bulb light up?

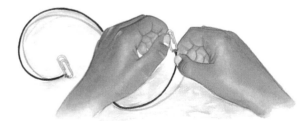

1 Take two pieces of electrical flex 20cm/8in long with bare ends. Wind each end around a paper clip.

4 Take the flex off one battery terminal. Is the bulb still lit?

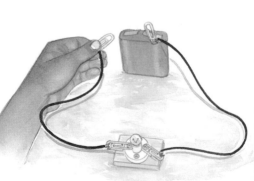

2 Clip a piece of flex to each battery terminal.

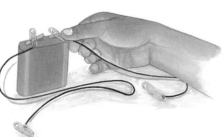

The bulb lights when the circuit is complete.

Keep it steady

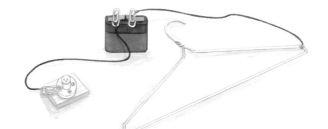

1 Remove one flex from your circuit. Attach a paper clip to one end of a piece of flex 25cm/10in long with bare ends. Clip the flex to the free battery terminal. Wind the other end round a metal hanger.

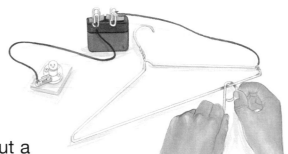

2 Put a piece of stiff wire 25cm/10in long through the middle of the hanger. Bend one end of the wire into a loop round the hanger.

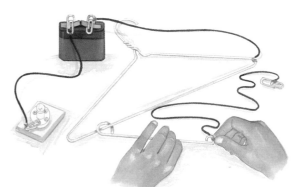

3 Get a piece of flex 40cm/15in long with bare ends. Twist one end of the flex around the free end of the stiff wire.

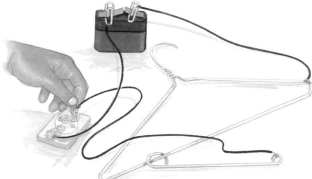

4 Attach the other end of this flex to the bulb holder. Hang up the hanger.

Try to pass the loop along the hanger without them touching. If the loop touches the hanger you will complete the circuit and the bulb will light up.

Stop or flow?

Electricity can only flow through certain materials. These are called **conductors**. Materials that do not let electricity flow through them are called **insulators**.

Light the bulb

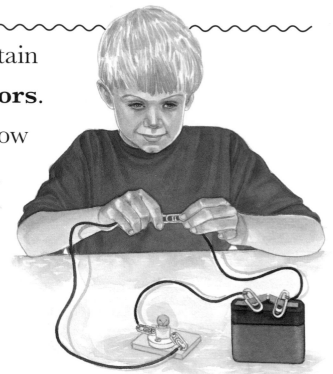

1 Set up a simple circuit as on page 24. Remove one flex from the bulb holder.

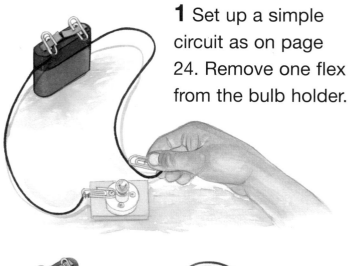

2 Get a piece of flex 15cm/6in long with bare ends. Put a paper clip on each end. Clip one end to the bulb holder. You should have two free ends of flex.

3 Touch the two paper clips together. The bulb should light up. If it doesn't, make sure all the connections are tight.

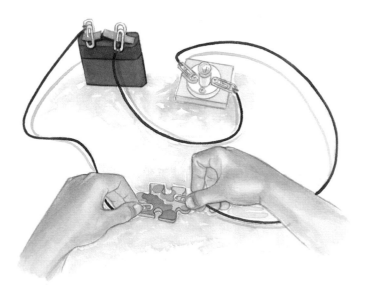

4 Put the two paper clips either side of a piece of wood. Touch the wood. Does the bulb light up?

You will need: 55cm/22in electrical flex, six paper clips, round-ended scissors, bulb, bulb holder, battery, objects made from plastic, cotton, wood, metal, cork and paper.

5 Collect a cork, a plastic brick, some kitchen foil, a coin, wood, nails, screws, drawing pins (thumb tacks) and paper clips. Test each material in turn. Which materials let the bulb light? Which do not?

Metals are conductors. They let the electric current through. The bulb lights up. Kitchen foil, paper clips, nails, screws and drawing pins are made of metal.

Wood, plastic and cork are insulators. They do not let electricity through, so the bulb does not light up.

On/off

When you switch off an electric light, the circuit is no longer complete. This means the bulb will not light. We can use a switch to turn any electrical circuit on and off.

You will need: 1m/1 yard electrical flex, four paper clips, round-ended scissors, battery, bulb, bulb holder, cardboard, sticky tape, bright paper, non-hardening clay, small jar, shallow cardboard box.

When you turn an electrical circuit on and off, you can make a light flash. A lighthouse does just that.

Flashing lighthouse

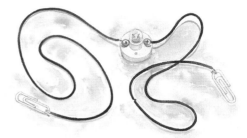

1 Fix two pieces of flex 40cm/15in long to a bulb holder. Put paper clips on the ends.

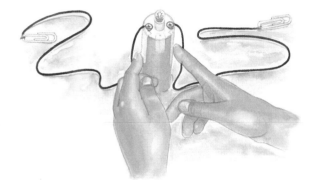

2 Roll some cardboard into a tube and tape it together. The bulb holder should just fit into the top of the tube. Tape it in place. The flex must be on the outside of the tube.

3 Tape the flex to the outside of the tube. Fix one flex to a battery terminal.

4 Get a piece of flex 20cm/8in long with bare ends.  Put paper clips on the ends. Fix one end of the flex to the free battery terminal. The two flexes with paper clips on the ends make a switch.

5 Cover the tube with some bright paper. Tape it in place. Stand the tube up in a box. Put clay around the bottom to make a base.

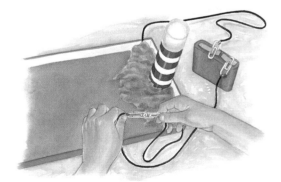

6 Put a small jar over the bulb. Now touch the two free paper clips. The bulb should light. Can you make the bulb flash on and off?

Hints to helpers

Pages 6 and 7

Only certain materials are magnetic. These include some metals, such as iron, nickel and cobalt, and alloys, such as steel. Talk about the uses of magnets, e.g. magnetic catches to keep things closed, compasses, machines for picking up metal.

The magnet will only attract the butterfly as long as it is within its magnetic field. When you move the magnet too far away from the butterfly it will fall back.

Pages 8 and 9

You can make your own magnets by stroking a magnet along a steel nail from the top to the tip. You should always stroke the nail in the same direction. Normally the tiny particles that make up the iron nail are pointing in different directions. As you stroke the nail with the magnet the particles form into lines pointing in the same direction. The nail will act as a magnet as long as the particles stay in line.

The magnets on the end of the stick attract the paper clips so that the fish are picked up. The magnetic force is not blocked by the water so a magnet can attract the paper clips even through water.

Pages 10 and 11

The magnetic force is not blocked by water, plastic or glass. It can still attract the metal drawing pins and paper clips.

Pages 12 and 13

Discuss how the Earth acts as if there is an enormous bar magnet down its middle. A compass needle is a small magnet and it lines up with the Earth's magnetic field so it always points north and south. Point out that the Earth's magnetic north and south poles are not quite the same as the geographic north and south poles shown on maps and globes.

The planes keep on swinging because the north poles repel each other, so the noses swing away from each other. This brings the tails together. The south poles also repel each other so the tails swing apart. The heads then swing together so the planes keep swinging. You can use the magnet with its poles marked red and green to find the north poles of your magnets for this experiment.

Pages 14 and 15

Explain that the Earth's magnetism comes from its inner core, which is made of the metals iron and nickel.

The vast magnetic force field around the Earth is called the magnetosphere. This traps electrically charged particles and so protects the Earth from the solar wind, a deadly stream of charged particles hurtling from the sun.

Pages 16 and 17

No one completely understands the invisible force that surrounds a magnet. The iron filings gather together in regions where the magnetic force is stronger. A lot of filings cluster at the ends of the magnet where the magnetic force is strongest.

The iron filings form lines between the north and south poles of two magnets because the magnetic fields between the poles join up. Opposite poles attract each other. The iron filings between two south poles bend away from the poles because the magnetic fields push away or repel each other.

Pages 18 and 19

Experiments with static electricity are most successful on dry, cold days. When the balloon is rubbed on the child's hair it gains tiny particles called electrons and develops a negative charge. The hair loses electrons and develops a positive charge. Just as the north and south poles of magnets attract each other, so a negative and a positive charge attract one another. The hair stands on end as it is attracted to the balloon.

When you rub the balloon with the nylon it becomes charged with static electricity. The charge on the balloon makes it stick to the wall. When the balloon is wet the static electricity cannot build up, so the balloon does not stick to the wall. Some materials, such as nylon and wool, build up a static charge very well. Others, like cotton and wood, do not.

A good way for a child to see and hear static electricity is by wearing a nylon shirt under a wool sweater. A static charge will build up between the sweater and the shirt. If you undress in a dark room and watch carefully in a mirror, as you pull off the jumper, you should hear a crackle and see some tiny sparks fly.

Pages 20 and 21

When the balloons are rubbed with the nylon, they both develop a negative charge. Equal charges repel each other so the two balloons push apart. When you rub the pen with nylon, the pen becomes charged and attracts

the tissue paper. The more you rub the pen, the greater the charge on it will be. If you wait, the charge on the pen will lessen and it will not attract the tissue paper so strongly.

Lightning is produced when static electricity builds up in a thundercloud. The top of the cloud becomes positively charged while the bottom of the cloud carries a negative charge. The negative charges are strongly attracted to the ground. They leap from cloud to cloud or to the ground as flashes of lightning. The heat from the flash makes the air expand suddenly making a loud thunder clap.

Pages 22 and 23

The picture of a kitchen shows a stovetop, whisk and food processor, all of which are powered by electricity. The weighing scales are not electric.

Discuss why all the parts of a torch (flashlight) are needed to make a complete circuit.

Pages 24 and 25

Discuss what happens when a circuit is complete. The electricity flows from the batteries through the wires to the bulb. If a wire is not connected the circuit is not complete so the electricity cannot flow to the bulb.

Pages 26 and 27

Discuss the use of conductors and insulators of electricity. For example, copper electric wires are good conductors. The plastic coverings on electrical wires are good insulators.

Discuss the uses of electrical switches in the home. For example, when you turn on a light, the switch closes a gap in the electrical circuit. This allows the current to flow through the bulb and light it. When you turn off the light, the switch opens the gap and breaks the circuit. So the electricity cannot flow and the bulb does not light.

Pages 28 and 29

The light can be made to flash on and off by touching or separating the paper clips and making or breaking the circuit.

Discuss other uses of flashing lights, such as security alarms, hazard lights etc.

Glossary

Attracts Draws or pulls towards. A magnet pulls magnetic objects such as iron or steel towards it.

Battery This has special chemicals inside it. They work together to make or store small amounts of electricity. A battery stops working when the chemicals are used up.

Circuit An electrical circuit is a path of wires. An electric current can only flow round the circuit when it is complete.

Compass An instrument with a needle that always points north–south. A compass helps you find your way. The needle is a magnet. Its tip is its north pole which always points to the north.

Conductors Materials that allow electricity or heat to pass through them, the opposite of insulators.

Electric charge An amount of electricity. There are two types of electric charge – a positive charge and a negative charge. Objects with opposite charges attract each other. Objects with the same electric charge repel each other.

Electric current A flow of electric charge through a material. Electricity flows through wires rather like water flows through a pipe.

Insulators Materials that do not allow electricity or heat to pass through them.

Lightning A huge spark of electricity that occurs during a thunderstorm. It is made when a static electric charge builds up in a cloud. The charge passes from cloud to cloud or from a cloud to the ground. We see it as a flash of light.

Magnetic field The space around a magnet in which the magnetic force can be felt.

Power station A building that makes electricity from other forms of energy such as coal and gas.

Repel To push away from. In magnets, it means the pushing apart of magnets when two like poles are brought near one another. This is called repulsion.

Static electricity A kind of electricity in which the electric charge stays still, or is static.

Switch An object that breaks or completes an electric circuit.